Some Things I Just Know
Poems About Life-Lessons Learned the Hard Way

By

Jackie Dove-Miller

Best Wishes!
Jackie
4-20-13

Jackie Dove-Miller

www.spiritofpeaceproducts.com

spiritofpeace2@gmail.com

First Edition

ISBN-13: 978-1482091946

ISBN-10: 1482091941

ACKNOWLEDGMENTS

To all those who have encouraged my poetic out-pourings —
thanks for believing in me: My parents, Eunice and H. Guy
Dove, Sr.; my siblings, Laurine Franklin, Janet Dail, Henry
Dove, Jr.; other family members, Catherine Murphy, Pearlie
Wilkie, Sherry Avery, Jeanette Hicks, Shiky Bolton; my friends,
Evelyn K. Harris, Ethel (Bunny) Evans, Daisy Mewborn, Linda
Rufus, and Barbara Long; my constant encouragers, Eugenia
Pleasants, Rona Leach, Eleanor Holder, Jameen Gude, Annette
Joyner-Moore, Joanie Jeffries; and friends who critiqued or
edited, Mary B. Smith, Delores Armstrong and Donna
Campbell Smith. Special thanks to the New Bethel Church
family, Savannah High School Alumni, 2nd Cup Writers, Page
Makers Writers.

A super special thank you to my husband Allen Miller, who
believes in me, my talented nephew, Terrence Dove (AKA
Brotha Soul) who provides the music for my poetry, and my
poetic muse, Minister Regelyn (Reggie) Edwards who believes
in my gift, inspires my writing and pushes me to challenge my
comfort zone. I love you all.

Thanks to anyone who came to hear me read, purchased my CD
or asked for printed copies of any of my poems. Your
encouragement has been invaluable.

DEDICATION

For all the participants of the Raleigh area Summer Camps for Women sponsored by Building Together Ministries and The Encouraging Place: May you continue moving forward with all your dreams of change. You are the best audience anyone could ask for.

I NEED TO GET NAKED

I need to get naked with you
To lay everything in the open
My baggage
My scars
My fears.
I need to wash off all make-up
So you can see how my past
Has marked my face
Leaving traces of pain
In the lines I try to cover.

I need to get honest
Say the words that have
Lingered around the edges
Of my tongue, their bitter
Trail crisscrossing my
Conversations with apologies
I shouldn't have to make
Lies I don't have to tell.

I need to expose
Every crack
Any space that holds a memory
A thought
A word
That has kept me
Walled within myself
Afraid someone will know
Who or what I've told myself
I am
And run away repulsed.

I need to strip bare
Empty out my heart
Dump its contents
Into the open air
And set it free
Snatching away the power to
Elicit fear from its
Iron fists so that
I can grip my heart
With both hands
And force its pumping
Into a rhythm that
Lulls my soul from its
Hiding place.

I need to
Peel the scabs from
Every wound to let them
Breathe…
Revealing what should have
Healed long ago
But hung like
Humid clouds
To make each breath
A chore.

I need to get naked
With you
So that the lies I tell myself
About who I am
Can be transformed into
The truth that lies trapped
Beneath all

I show the world.
Then, I can stand naked
In front of my own soul's
Mirror
And see my divine,
Eternal worth.

CONNECTIONS

We feel artificially linked
Since so many differences
Appear.
Yet when we strip away
The paint
And decorations,
At our soul's core
We are the same—
Linked to each other
By experience
By need
By carnal desires.
We stand alone
Out of fear
That our difference
Signals our
Unwanted otherness
Though we long
For connection
A touch that says
Come—
Help me choose
How to use this life-space,
How to save this breath,
How to find real joy.
When we acknowledge
Our soul's connection
Everything beautiful
Can grow.

I AM

Anyone who brings news
That changes our view
Of who we are
And what is good
Is seen by the masses as
A threat.
Don't want to hear
That we can be better
Don't want to believe
What we do is less than
What God asks.
Every Messiah
Martyrs his life
Yet tells his truth
Despite those who
Refute it.
No danger stops his rush to do
That which his spirit says
He must.

Christ was hushed
But spoke again
Through the voices
Of those who woke
To his message.
His declaration
I am that I am, meant
I am whom you see
I am the person God
Meant me to be

I am all I've agreed
With my father I'd be
When in spirit
He chose to send me
Here.

I am the I am,
And
That which is in me
Is from God.
Christ reminds me
God made me who I am.
Not made in China,
India or Japan
I was breathed into
By the Greatest I AM.
That means I won't chip
Or crack
Under the Pressure of life.
I won't break in heat
Or warp in rain.
Wind may blow me off course
But I will ride
On the breath of God
And thus will make it home.

Christ brought the news
That who we are
Is perfect.
Life steals that
Knowledge—
Makes us
Ashamed

Fills our minds with
Doubt.

But today
That message is reprogrammed:
Christ's spirit in me confirms that
I too am that I am.

IT'S ALL ABOUT ME

Today,
It's all about me.
I'm not pretending any more.
I pulled on my *big girl panties*
And headed out the door!

My attitude signaled everyone
To leave me alone
I've finally realized
After far too long —
I'm grown.
I am no longer tending to
Everyone else's needs.
Today is a self-love day,
So, I'm just focusing on me.

I've stepped out of that chameleon shell
Being what others want me to be
Starting today, I'm moving straightway
Into the truth of me.

No more holding my peace
So he won't get mad.
No more tagging along
Becoming her walking pad.
No more hiding my needs
Running almost on empty
No more denying my dreams,
Neglecting my "Me."

Today, I'm speaking up for me
Telling others what I see,
Loving that image in the mirror
Because it's the true unadulterated me.

That's why I left the house make-up free...
No mask of perfection necessary— just me.
All those years spent hiding,
Painting on a smile for others to see.
I'd squeeze the God within so tight
All others could see was the faintest,
Faintest light.

But not today.

Today, I'm stepping forth
A new creature in Christ...
No— a new creature, Christ-in
Through whom I can do all things.

No insecurity, or doubt, no fear of rejection
My goals will be reached
According to God's perfection.

Those people who cling on
Trying to drag me down
Those who speak negativity
Will no longer be around.
I'm through trying to be all things
To all people
Am taking time out just to do me.

I've got things to do to fulfill my dreams
Prayers to pray, affirmations to speak
There are roads to travel and mountains to climb
Even in valleys-low, I know I can still shine.
Because I know who I am
Know what's simmering within…
The spirit of God
Against which others can form no weapon.

So, finally, it's all about me.
I've held back too long
Let life get me down
But today I'm taking control
I've turned things around
As of today, I am walking a new way:
My back is straighter, my head tilted high
I'm lifting my feet lighter
Because I'm about to fly.

And my super-hero cape …
Well, I've packed that away
But you need not distress—
I've traded it in for a sexy red dress!

I WAS BORN FOR GREATNESS

I was born for greatness!
At home
At play
On the job.
I didn't pray for greatness
I was a thought in the mind
Of God.

So when troubles came
Singing rain's refrain
I kept the faith that
God's master plan
Was for my good
And each rainfall would be
Understood by and by.

I felt my greatness
But when people thought
I ought to conform
I questioned
I doubted
I searched and cried
I wondered about
The passion inside—
If it was truly God's gift
Given me to uplift
Forgetting that the door
At which I only stood
Was opened long before
By the shedding of blood.

So I sat on my talents
Instead of soaring like I should.

But again…
God called me to greatness
And I believed.
He breathed my name
Planned my game
And cleared the lane for
My success.

So, instead of wallowing in
Life's pain
I stood and claimed
My resurrection.
Tearing myself from the trap of fear
Freeing my mind from the grip of doubt
And finally stepping out
On the premise that
If I was born to be great
I'd better get started
And stop these half-hearted
Attempts
At fitting in—
Content with
Mediocrity.

To claim my greatness
I let go the façade
That choice was involved
No! I KNOW
My greatness was destined
As a thought in the mind of God.

WALKING ON WATER

The dream that's bubbling within me
Is aching to be set free
But I'm rooted in fear
Grounded in doubt
And stuck in complacency.

The storms that plague my brave attempts
To finally take a step
Reinforce my fears that I might fail
And lose my self-respect.

I stand on the shallow banks
Of what seems an uncrossable sea
But God sends a rainbow message:
Just step out confidently.

Since Jesus walked on water
Preacher says I can too.
I just need to be brave enough
To test what faith can do.

I don't believe I can walk on water
So I begin to sink
Not realizing God's plan for me
Is bigger than I can think.

EVERYTHING BEGINS WITH A THOUGHT

Life's journey begins amidst smiles
And joy
The world awaits our arrival
The early years are free of care
And all that we dream is possible.

But while we grow we hear the tales
Of all that we can not be
Since society is not really designed
For women like you and me.

The models we see aren't leading
Businesses—
They work hard in the church.
They choose men who don't carry
Their weight
Or who hit them when they themselves
Hurt.

Nobody told our mothers to follow their dreams
Nobody thought they could
Nobody pointed out their magnificent gifts
Nobody praised their good.
So our moms taught us the same old "shoulds."

But some of us now don't believe what we were taught
Especially that negative stuff
We've pushed back the clouds that covered our dreams
We've listened to the No's long enough.

Our fancy turns to dreams unnourished
Inspiration is caught.
Belief ignites—ideas flame
New life begins with that thought.

Like a single leaf's flutter signals the
Coming of fall
In a gust of wind it gets caught
Reminding us gently what we've come to know
Every change begins with a thought.

We know to surround ourselves
With people who'll help
Those who care that we thrive.
We've made our decision—
We've done the prep
Now, our journey to greatness
Begins with one step.

GRACE PAID FORWARD

When we speak
Negatively about others
We don't really want someone
To show us our error
Or
Direct us toward a different point
Of view.
We want to believe
The noise we make
Though we wouldn't stake
Our lives on its truth.
We may not even
Believe what we've said.
We just want to
Feel superior.
We want the person
Being talked about
To be — for that moment—
Unworthy in someone's
Eyes.
When I'm
Within earshot.
My job is to listen
And agree
And perhaps tell someone else
So I too can feel better to a degree.

I don't like that game
So I just keep giving
My point of view
Only to be chewed out

For not agreeing
For not knowing
The person like they do
For not having a clue.

But I think I do.
Since I believe we're being
Small minded
When we discuss
Other people's junk:
Their loud clothes,
Bad children,
Jacked-up hair-does,
Bounced checks,
Baby daddies,
Split verbs
Run-over shoes,
And raggedy cars
Not knowing the stories behind
Most of our gossip.

We think the
Venom we spew
Takes the focus off of us
For a few seconds
But our subconscious is really
Confessing our own
Inadequacies.

Telling other people's business
Is the one way we
Can shine —
Can point an accusing
Finger away from

Our low self-esteem
By naming their sins
Though their bad behaviors don't
Begin to compare
To ours.

Small minds discuss people
In small ways
Never holding the mirror
Up to our own faces
Or praying that some trace of pain
Reflected in our sister's behavior
Be healed.

I won't stop playing
Devil's advocate
Once I peek that small minded game
Because
Giving a sister
Open heart-space
Is my way of thanking God
For His daily Grace.

If I can face my sister's pain
Without judgment
God will erase the stains of my past.
If His grace is sufficient for me
Then who am I to disagree that
My sister deserves the same?

TRUE POWER

I have the power
To change a life
Sometimes
With a smile
Sometimes with
A word
Sometimes just by
Saying,
I understand.

I have the power
To create a world
Where
Someone knows
He matters
Someone knows
She counts
Someone knows
He is enough—
Just the way he is
Because I shared
My deeper,
Truer, more loving
Self—
And made life
Better
For us both.

FREE WILL

God gives us
Free will
To live all the days
He has planned
Or lose ourselves to the
Dark melancholy
Set in so long ago
We can't remember
Its source…
Only the deep hole
Left
Where God would dwell
If we let Him.

God won't stop us from choosing
Death
Over His comfort,
But He will offer alternatives:
He will remind us of His power
Through the healing of disease.
He'll remind us of life's joy
Through the love and care of family.
He will offer us peace
In the whispers to our hearts
To let us know He'll light the way
Through our dark places
Carry us over rough waters
Or free us of whatever
Binds our spirits.
But He will not stop us
If we choose eternity's sleep
Over a restful heart.

Ponder this:
How can we pray,
Thy will be done,
While making choices
To the contrary?

Warning:
God will not choose
His will over our own.
In the end,
He will step aside
And let us die.

DESPERATION IS A TERRIBLE PERFUME TO WEAR

Desperation is a terrible perfume to wear
It demands too much struggle in too little a room
It causes feelings of hopelessness and extreme despair
Its tainted air suffocates and consumes.

The odor of need fills the surrounding air
It follows the wearer into every room
She makes believe that she doesn't care
But her desperation predicts her doom.

Anxiety seeps from pores and hair
Others smell the stench of too much need
In her overwhelming desire and despair
Her perfume reeks of lust and greed.

Despondency over a relationship she can't repair
He's moved on and left her for good
Now desperation is the only perfume she wears
Since her whole life is one big falsehood.

The stench of desperation trails her everywhere
She pretends she doesn't recognize the smell
But others see her extreme despair
And the traps of hopelessness into which she fell.

She can mask the emptiness with smiles and flair
But the stench of desperation still fills the room
Desperation is a terrible perfume to wear
It's the curse of hopelessness and undisguised despair.

LOVE'S REFLECTIVE POWER

Real love makes you look
At yourself
Check behind the
Motives
Meanings
And mumblings
For ego-centered
Mutterings
That hurt
Or shamed
The other.
It pushes you to be
Better today than
Yesterday
When you found
Your selfish nature
Unable to hear
The fear
Behind the other's
Anger or
To see his mask
A camouflage of pain.

Real love makes you
Check yourself
For behaviors
To which you
Cling
Despite the
Current situation
And
Share the truth

That the thing he said
Triggered
A memory that
Stung your heart—
Not him.
It makes you search
For truth
In all you give
So that the other
Knows you
At your best
And when
Your worst looms big
He sees
Beyond the storm cloud
Knowing the rainbow
That is your true
Nature will arc
In minutes.

Real love
Makes you look in
Your soul's
Mirror
Uncover the layers
Of junk you've
Hidden
Blow the dust off
Past failures and fears
And stare them down
Declaring their hold on you
Forever broken
Since now you see

Yourself through
The other's eyes
And he sees
Only beauty.

Real love frees you to
Live the highest expression
Of your flawed but
Growing self.
It makes you want to find
God within
So all you give
The other
Is holy.

THE POWER OF FEAR

Fear is powerful—
It Intimidates.
Its internal dialogue
Fosters self-hate.

That self-hate lies—
Tells us we can't
Keeps us wound tight
So we don't
See our inner light.

Self–hate and Fear
Walk hand in hand
They value fluff
Not the stuff that heals.

Fear's negativity and
Self-hate's reign
Is only a cover-up
For unresolved pain.

But fear,
Touched by love
Grows quickly tired
Always mired
In a shadow-life.
It makes a plan
To stand against
Negativity and doubt.

Once the plan is made
Love is unafraid
Of freedom
Knowing she can rise
From the dust
Of self-doubt and mistrust.

Love knows that once
My intent is to seriously try
I'll grow more courage
And begin to fly.
My colors will shine
My heart will grow
My beauty will awe
And all will know
That love's power
Is real.

I've done my work
And broken through
Away from fear
Into something brand new
A life of doing what is right
Moving from fear's darkness
Into love's marvelous light.

Love's work is done in stillness
For change requires inward sight
First comes the breakthrough—
A flutter—
Then flight.

Love and fear
Can't co-exist
For darkness and light
Can never mix.
Their power seems equal
Until love tiptoes in
With fear's loss of control
Walking in purpose can begin.

Once light conquers
It becomes quite clear
All that's not love
Is unnecessary fear.

FOR MY GOOD

Life's chilly winds blew fiercely
And I had to stand them alone
But a fire started inside me
And my will to survive grew strong.

I stood at the foot of a mountain
Afraid I could not make the climb
But each step forward made me stronger
And I grew sure-footed over time.

Some days were long and lonely
Dark clouds sometimes hung overhead
I thought the dark would consume me
But I learned to see through it instead.

What seemed obstacles to my success
Became my stepping-stones
They forced me to hone my personal skills
So I could soar on my own.

A mountain, dark days, a chilly wind
Could have pushed me back like the tides
But when times began to overwhelm
I looked to the power inside.

That's what God calls surrender—
Acknowledging my servant-hood
Then God can use my obstacles
In His plan designed for my good.

FORGIVENESS

Ok, I forgive you.
Although you disrespected me
Dismissed my needs
Disavowed my intellect
And dehumanized my personhood
I forgive you.

The preacher says that I need to forgive
Because there is healing there.
And I do need to be healed
From the deep scars left by your harsh words
From the emptiness left by your neglect
From the confusion created by your
Thinking you know what is best for me
When you have yet to learn me at my core.
I need to heal from the loneliness
Caused by feeling abandoned
The self-doubt caused by feeling abused
And the self-destruction caused by
Being made to feel unworthy.
Oh, yeah. I need to heal
So I'm forgiving you.

The preacher implies that
With healing comes peace
Which means there is peace in forgiveness
A sense of well-being and safety—
Like I got when sitting quietly beside my mother
While watching TV or shelling peas as a child

Breathing in her goodness and knowing
That she would die to save my life
Or that confidence I felt the first time I crossed
The street alone in front of on-coming traffic
Because my daddy had taught me how.
Forgiveness provides that type of safety net.
It opens the airways for God's messages
To get through to a receptive vessel—
The human heart.
To put it in a theological place:
Forgiveness is the passageway to Grace.
Maya and Oprah have said, *When you know better,*
Your responsibility is to do better.
So that's why I have to forgive,
Because I do know better now.
I know I need the healing, the peace, and even the
freedom
That come with forgiving.

So, this poem is for the X's and Y's of my life:
My ex-boyfriends, my ex-husband, my ex-friends—
Friends who forced me to question WHY;
Why use me, lie to me, steal from me?
Why show me one side of your personality to gain
entrance to my heart
Then morph into some alien creature once entrenched
there?
This poem is for all those who have been inconsiderate
Of my time
My needs
And my love .

Even me.

Yes…
Today, I'm forgiving me too—
Because I rushed headstrong into life
Not trying to balance my needs against your wants
Because I gave myself away to a relationship
That was too unhealthy to thrive in
That implied that I was to blame
For everything wrong in the world
Because I stopped defending my sense of self
And questioned my value as a human being
I questioned my beauty
My intelligence
My business acumen
My creative genius
My natural leadership ability
My love of adventure
And my ability to stand in the face of fear.
Can you imagine that?
I questioned a masterpiece.
I questioned God's craftsmanship.
I questioned the passion bubbling inside me
And wondered if it were worth pursuing
Even though God put it there.
My actions said that God must have been on vacation
During my creation.
Did I think I could do better?
Did I think YOU knew better?

I must have because I listened to you sinister-sing
Though God was ceaselessly whispering,
You are wondrously and fearfully made.
I still closed myself away from HIS voice,
And let your choices, that stole my strength, mean more.

That behavior REQUIRES forgiveness.
So, today, I forgive ME... and I forgive you.
I forgive, not because what you did was okay
Nor because I chose the right way.
But because I need to be released from
The bondage of unforgiveness
So that I can appreciate the wonder
And the beauty
That is me.

THE GAME OF LIFE

As the ball bounces
So go my chances
Of rising high
Above my
Current circumstances
Filling myself with
Knowledge
Instead of hot air
Making positive choices
To show I care
About who I can be.

The ball is tossed into
My court.
Destiny is the referee,
But the game winning shot
Is left up to me.

ONE STEP AT A TIME

They say
If you take one step,
God will take two…
Times as many as required
To help you make it through.

I took one step today
So small some might not
Call it a step at all.
But the important thing
Is that I did not fall.

One step begets the
Thought of two
And after that
You can view yourself
Actually doing the thing.

And since I stood
It felt so good
I thought it must be true
To overcome my fear
Of falling
I'd have to try for two.

The thought of two
Renewed my fear;
I stood there petrified
But after one breath in
And a quick exhale
I closed my eyes
And tried.

Success felt sweet
I savored it
My wings began to sprout
They gave me brand new
Confidence
And drove my fear right out.

I had told myself I had no skill
I couldn't get it right
But I took a step
Despite my fear
And then I thought I might.

My wings were spread
I said a prayer
Affirming God's plan for me
With arms outstretched and faith
As wind,
I attempted step number three.

One— wiggle
Two—wobble
Three—I hit the floor.
But two successes
Let me know that I
Truly wanted more.

And so, I asked for help.

Out from the clamoring den
Of inspiring voices
Came friends
Who applauded my positive choices
Who grabbed each hand

And helped me stand
In support of my master plan.

One said, Yes, just take that step.
The other nodded and smiled.
And that's all that I needed
To believe
I could now walk a mile.

Step one
Then two, then three
I let my fear shake free
And with the cheers of friends
I felt God carry me.

That's when I recalled
Philippians 1:6,
He who began a good work in you
Will carry it on to completion, says Paul
Assuring me that when I take the right steps
God won't let me fall.

They say if you take one step
God will surely take two
He'll manifest in teams and friends
Who'll open doors for you.

SURRENDER

I walked up to the door
And knocked
But was stopped by fear—
Was blocked by years of
Hearing NO.

I closed my ears
Shut out the voices
And pushed.
It didn't budge.

But this is my calling, I cried.
Why can't I get to the other side?
Why does each door seem the right one
But then nothing ever comes
Of my walking through?

A tiny voice answered,
Here's what you must do:
Surrender.
But I still didn't have a clue
So I knocked again
With no success.
Then threw up my hands
As if saying, I'm done,
And a new thing was begun
In me.
I felt a shifting of my soul—
A burden released
I sensed an inner knowing,
And my faith increase

Immediately I knew
God was now in control.

What surrender looks like—
I don't know
But it feels like a letting go
A giving in
A voluntary bend at last
After trying to push the world around
On its circuitous path
What surrender shows is
That I certainly don't know—
Can't figure it out
Have released all doubt that
I can not do this alone
Can't do it at all if I don't call
On God to work it out.

In undulating silence,
Within the noisy swill
Unuttered words ascend,
Not mine, but God,
Do Your will.

WHO I AM ALONE

Sitting on idle
While life whooshes by
Just can't get myself
In gear—
Can't try.
Wish things weren't
This way
Wish my life hadn't
Turned so strange.
But it is what it is
And I don't have the energy
To change.

I can't explain the emptiness
I feel
Can't foresee that it
Will ever heal.
But the real truth is
He's gone
And I don't know
How
I'll carry on.
Don't know who I am
Alone.

SELF-LOVE

To thine own self be true
But how can you
If you don't know you?
And how can you know you
When all your internal images
Are encrypted
From the slip-ups
The trip-ups and the mix-ups
Of your youth?

So, self-love is not easy
It's difficult to come to
One must quell the nagging voices
Of youth that daily haunt you.

Voices that hacked at your self-esteem
And backed you into a corner of self-doubt
That sing-song
All but sing-along:
If you're dark… you can't
If you're fat… you can't
If you're slow… you can't
Too tall
Too short
Too poor… you can't
If your uncle
Or brother or daddy
Touched you where and how he shouldn't have
You can't come back from that.
Can't love a self that's soiled
Can't love a self that's embroiled
In the black of pain.

So, self-love comes through
Crisis…
From hitting bottom
But not death
Being thrust
Into the void of silence
Where all that is left is breath.

In the silence we can
Hear God's whisper:
I love you; now stand up.
And if we heed His message
He will surely
Fill our cups.

Within that cup of fullness
Still void of daily sounds
We come to know God's loving pull
From lost into the found.

We learn that even in spite of us
God still finds delight in us.
Had Jeremiah to write to us:
Before I formed you
I knew you.
In the womb,
I approved of you…
How can we not then love
What is already loved above?

So, self-love is first love
Though it seldom comes in youth
It finds us first upon our knees
In a humbling search for truth.

Self-love comes from knowledge
Of who you are amid the crowd
Or in the solitude of oneness
When that inner voice speaks loud.

In crisis we are forced to yield
To the hand with strength divine
He leads us to what's constant
Showing us we're meant to shine.

Then self-love starts to draw boundaries
Standing strong on what you will
Not do
Not allowing anyone to
Lead or manipulate you.

It fills you up and warms you
Though food and heat are nil
It's that internal knowing
That, that within fulfills.

Self-love then illuminates
One's aura shines aglow
Like God flipped on your
Eternal switch
Letting all your golden show.

Self-love helps us overcome
Frees us to finally feel
It points us to what's truly real
Then we can start to heal.

Yes, self-love
Heals
And self-love shields us from the one
Who seeks to
Steal, or kill.

And through the healing
We start to see that thing
That could be thought odd:
Self-love comes from the realization
That we are first loved by God.

FEAR OF SUCCESS

I used to think I was afraid of
Success
But that made no sense.
Who wouldn't want to soar
If she could touch
The clouds and
Shine like stars?
I found the paradox
Perplexing.

Fear of change—
Moving from comfort
To uncertainty
Into a new self
Where I might not
Feel at home
And where others
Might not know me.

So,
There it was—
The old question
That plagued my youth
And stunted my growth…
Would anyone love me
If they saw my wings?

Finally, I heard God whisper:
Those who really love
Will love you still
And if they don't
Be assured, that I always will.

I have things for you to do—
A word of love to spread.
I'll open doors and wait inside
You shouldn't be afraid.
If you get more material wealth—
If you let me help you fly
That will be your just reward
But I'll be glorified.

THAT SOMETHING WITHIN

There is something within me
That is strong enough
To keep me from toppling
Over the edge of sanity
Over the ledge of frustration
Or over the hedge of
All-out foolishness.
It leads me to prayer
When I would otherwise break.

There is something in my make-up
Or perhaps my bringing up
Or just the way I look up
That straightens my back
And bows my head.
It becomes the focus of my meditation
The sentiment in my supplication
The reason for my transformation.
That thing within me
Has me choosing light
Though darkness covers all.
It wells up like ocean waves
Come to drown those who
Think they deserve to push me back
Hold me down or
Steal my joy.
I have a spiritual strength that
Grows deeper and speaks louder
As I get to know
More about who I am.

Where did IT come from? Someone recently asked.
I answered, In my developing stage,
Someone said out loud,
You sure are good at _____.
My puny soul embraced that seed,
And it planted itself deep inside me and took root.
I tested that tiny bit of ego-strength against
The negative messages my family used to focused on
What I was NOT good at, making me feel small
And disconnected.

I was NOT good at being like my mother
Who was all but saintly.
I was NOT good at being
Like my sister, who was beautiful and dainty.
I was NOT ballerina thin or prissy neat,
But I WAS good at _____
And when I looked a little further,
I discovered —
I was GOOD ENOUGH.
Good enough to bear fruit
And reap a harvest
Good enough plant seeds
In others and watch them grow
Magnificent and free.
I was GOOD ENOUGH to relate to
The GOD that's inside of me.

So, this poem is for all my sister-friends
Who don't yet know that
We are better than what our mothers,
Our teachers, the men in our lives,
Or even the good sisters in church have called us.

Because God has called us blessed
And HIS is the only voice that matters.

So, here and now, I pray our sister-prayer:
Dear Lord,
Help me to release
The self-doubt
That lives in my heart.
Remind me daily
That I am the product of
Your hands…
And all that you make
Is Perfect.
Amen.

HIDDEN SCARS

Sometimes I think
My soul is marred.
My wounds are so deep
My heart so scarred
Can't be healed
Until I can feel
God's love for me is real.

Scar One:
He said he loved me
But he lied
Had several women
On the side.
But I stayed.
Made myself close my eyes
Lost both my pride and self-esteem.
Now I have deep scars
I hide for life
And live with the label
The betrayed wife.
Can't love again until
I begin to see myself
Through God's eyes.

Scar Two:
He'd come home late
And full of rage.
No matter what hateful thing
He said
I was always afraid to talk back
Or stand my ground…
Or the morning found me

With a black eye or swollen lip.
He always found a way to
Shift the blame…
Made me ashamed to want
To flee
And I stayed …
Afraid to fight back
Afraid to walk free
Hopeless that happiness
Would ever find me.
Can't live again till I begin
To trust God to take care of me.

Scar Three:
My mother called me ugly
Said I was too chubby
To run and play
So I had to stay
Cooped up inside
To hide from others' stares.
No one cared that I was
A treasure of gold
So I believed the lies I was told
And saw myself through their eyes
Never valuing my gifts
Never shifting my thoughts
Or living without doubt.
Can't love myself until I
Can feel God move in.

Scar Four:
He raped me.
I didn't know it was
Rape at the time

But it was.
I didn't say no
But I didn't say yes
Either:
His hand under my dress
On my breast
All over—
Inside me.
He pushed and pushed
Till my scream pierced his
Consciousness.
Then he looked at me—
Finally saw my humanness
And ran.
He just took what
He wanted
And ran.

He raped me.
Defiled my sacredness
Entered me there
But left the memory of his sweat
And the heat of his breath
Imprinted on my soul
Broke the image of myself
Into pieces so tiny I may never
Be whole again.
Looking out from eyes that can no longer see beauty
Mirrored there
I say a prayer for the little girl
I used to be
Before he raped me.
Can't be clean again until God washes me.

Life dealt us some crushing blows.
We assumed we'd easily outgrow the pain,
But our scars are too deeply rooted
Too staunchly engrained.
Can't let go …until we know
God's love.

BETTER THAN MY PAST

I am better than my past—
Better than the last
Bad thing I did
Because I am not that thing.

I am not that thought
That might not have been so nice
Or that word that twice got me in trouble.
I am not that act
That made my family frown.
Am not the garbage from my past
In which I could have drowned.

I am not just my secrets
Not just the things I regret
I am not just the behaviors
I'd rather forget.

I am not my tears,
My fears,
Or the years lost
To behaviors
I'd rather not remember.

I am the sum total of all that and more:
My memories— good and bad,
My experiences—happy and sad,
My conversations — hostile or sweet,
My interactions — dull or unique,
My heart breaks — with all their lessons,
My joy compounds — with all their blessings.

I am each person I have touched
And each whose heart touched me
I am all the ideas I've questioned
And those with which I've agreed.

I am all that I've done
All that I've seen
All that I've loved
And all that I've dreamed.

I am better than I think
Better than others know
For with each painful lesson
My soul so deeply grows.

Every breath
Every tear
Every heartbeat
Has brought me here
Wrapped in layers of
Comfort
Dusty from life's winding
Road
Steeped in the joy of knowing
The rainbow
The nectar
And the sublime and contented soul
All come at a cost
So nothing is ever lost
If I'm refined like gold.

No, I don't regret my past
Because every last event
Was aligned by God.
He used each step, each path
I trod
To teach me about His love.

That's why
Now…
I'm better than my past
Since the last bad thing I did
God wiped clean
So I could begin again
And become what He
Intended.

OFF WITH THE BACK PACK

I've got stuff on my back
That weighs me down
Stuff I carry
From years ago.

There are memories
Of hurts
Lies and
Neglect
Tucked in crevices of my
Heart
I no longer visit.
It just occupies space
But could be fertile ground
For unmeasured Grace.

There are names
Dates and
Places
That stir up my pain
That play out like
Movies
That leave me ashamed:
The Green Mile of envy
Of friends who have more
The Hurt Locker of Tears
Where I keep my pain stored.

I've got old troubles
Old disappointments
Mistakes and bad choices

And I've got negative
consequences
That all but destroyed me.

I spent years *Waiting to Exhale*
Because some man
Didn't see my worth
And I
Broke under the pressure
Of others'
Inconvenient Truths.

I hold on to this stuff—
Carry it around
And I blame its weight
For keeping me bound

But the truth is…
I'm afraid to let it all go.
Afraid I'll accidentally grow
Big, **new** dreams
I'll have to forego.
So, instead of my wall of
Memories keeping me safe
I've cultivated my anger
And developed self-hate.

Plus, my stuff keeps me from tipping
Forward into the unknown.

But what if tipping forward
Would send me into
Fertile Territory
Ripe with possibility?

What if that Power which lies
Dormant within
Could be freed to grow
If I just let go
Of all that I
Needlessly carry
From so long ago?

What if I
Lay down this backpack
Of bad memories—
Bind that fear and anger,
And put on a robe of faith?
What if I set myself free?
What then would be loosed
In Heaven
Meant just for me?

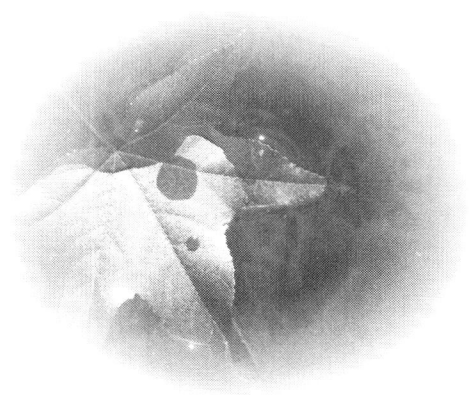

CO-DEPENDENCY

I can't do this anymore
Can't keep opening my door
To your drama.
I can't calm your fears
Can't wipe your tears
Can't pay that one bill
The day they say they'll
Cut it off or put you out.
Cut off the power
Cut off the phone
Cut off the cable
If you're not able to pay today.
I can't keep bailing you out
At my expense.
Heck I can barely afford
My own rent
And yet, I'm asked again
And again to lend my last cent
So that you can hang on
Another month.

I can't do this anymore.
Can't round up the forces
To support your melt down
Because that man just won't
Do right.
Won't help pay the bills
Won't help with the kids
Won't half come home at night.
Your anger implodes,
Pushing him to explode
And just as before, there's a fight.

And here you come
Knocking at my door
Knowing I'll take you in.
The family rallies round—
Running all over town
Protecting you from that man
Again.
And what do you do?
Go right back when things calm down.

I know I'm to blame
For your reckless behavior.
Afterall
I couldn't let you fall.
Reacted every time you'd call
Couldn't see I had become
Your enabler.
I'd rush to your aid
Make sure bills got paid
And let you use me
Despite it all.

But…
I can't do it anymore.
I've got to let you go
Gotta start saying no
So that you can grow—
Grow up
Grow strong
Grow a spine… or a heart
Or a brain.
Whichever it takes to help you see

That you can't keep living
In survival mode.

I can't do this anymore
Can't be your safety net
Because in all my giving
I never really get.
Can't get no peace
Can't get no love
Can't get to breathe free
With you depending on me.
And me depending on you
To add a spark to my day
By needing me to do
That one more thing
Just one more time—
Right now
Before your world falls down.
I won't do it any more
As of today…
I love you—but you're on your own.

THE GIFT OF REJECTION

I don't love you anymore…
Remember when Teddy sang that tune
And we danced
And sang along?
Our hips moved
Our feet grooved
And we gave no thought to
The girl he'd left behind.
She was not us
So we sweated out our curls
To her pain.
Then it happened to us.
Some handsome young man
With tight buns and chiseled abs
Said those words to each of us
Ending a dance we thought
We could do
Better than most.
His words flashed us back
To all the rejections of our past
All the relationships that did not last
All the times we felt cast aside,
Making us want to run and hide because
We were not
Good enough.

It starts early, you know:
A mother who expects perfection
Sets her girl child up to perceive rejection
A father who ignores his only son
Sets him on a course to feel loved by no one
And the pain gets internalized as

Who we are.
So, despite being grown
We still own that pain
And "I don't love you anymore"
Echoes from daddy
And mama,
Teacher,
And friend,
And every other lover who
Walked away in the end.
"I don't love you anymore"
Rewinds the tape
That reminds us
Nobody ever did.

But in the quiet of my heart
A tiny voice starts
First in a whisper
Then a shout
I love you enough
To have died for you
I love you   enough
I   love you.

A fire ignites within my soul
It burns so brightly
I start to feel whole.
And the face in the mirror
Looks brand new
It glows
From knowing what I

Can do
For my inner child
Who feels not enough:
Create my own encouraging tune—
A new and powerful staccato song
Sung thumping-loud and hip-bumping strong
No matter who walks away.

I can sing, *I love me some me*
And live the truth within those words.
'Cause that man's rejection
Can not undo
God's love or his intended perfection.

Rejection has taught me
A lesson
And strengthened my resolve
To live on the sacred promise
I am always enough for God.

I WANT TO MATTER

I want to matter!
Despite what I look like,
Or where I live
How poor I am, how fat I am or my
Skin tone…
Despite my kinky hair or my balding head,
How stooped my shoulders,
Or if I'm well read.
Even though I may not speak with eloquence
Or have ten extraordinary talents
I want my presence on this earth to matter
To at least one other human being!

I want one friend to see my soul
And to be joyful that God hand-selected me
To be in her life to lock at least one
Puzzle-piece into place
So that her life-picture is one inch more complete.
I want her spirit to connect with mine like it did
Before we chose these bodies to be human in.

I want someone to know my heart…
To see beyond the stoic exterior
And view the love
That bubbles just below the surface
But burrows as deep as the bones.

I want someone to want to know me—
To care about my hurts
To listen to my story's rendering
And still want to be there
For its ending.

66

I want him to need me at his core
Like breath... and pulse... and blood.

Each of us has that need—to matter
To know that our lives count for more
Than this flesh we live in
Flesh that turns to dust in the end.
So, this poem is for all those who
Don't yet feel their own value—
Who walk through life unaware
That God has placed purpose there
In the soul—
That only we can fulfill
That He has implanted genius
In each of us—
Either one talent or ten,
And NO ONE comes here empty-handed.
We each bring to life SOMETHING that
someone else needs
To know, to have, or to heed.

To those with whom we share our true selves
We do matter.
We are BUT matter when we lie.
When we pretend to be hard, but our core is soft...
When we pretend to be competent but we ought
To ask for help...
When we are lost or lonely,
Weak or afraid,
And do not say out loud,
"This is who I am!"
We can not matter
For no one can taste our essence

Through frosting, thick and rich,
But full of empty calories.

In short: it is our truth that matters
For our truth is our connection to the divine
Our truth is how God shines
Through us.
So, we matter when we bring our true selves,
broken or healed,
To the table, and feast as though it were prepared in
our honor.
Yes, we matter when we can look into our own eyes
And see God's reflected smile.

So, despite what the world uses to dismiss me,
Be it age, or gender, race, or looks—
In this moment, let the beauty of my truth
Flow forward as I thank God for reminding me
That revealing my true self
Is what matters most.

I, A WOMAN

I, a woman,
Am valid
And worthy—
The by-product of
My humanness
Because I was born into
This life
With breath
And thoughts
And the ability to
Create.

I, a woman,
Look only within.
After years of searching
I find that
That which is
Inside my spirit
Is the truth of
My strength
The source of my
Guidance
The beginning of
My power.
That ember of knowing
Ignites into wisdom.
That inkling of love
Flames into compassion
And I stand—
Resisting the urge
To look away
Pulling on courage

As though it were
My robe of many colors
And run straight into
Purpose
Fulfilling that which my
Father calls me to do:
To walk
Humbly.
I run straight
Into my
Destiny: Greatness.

I honor that greatness
By living my best
And letting the rest
Of life's pettiness
Evaporate
Like dew.
I bask in renewal
By looking within
By listening within
By living within
The confines of my Father's
Plans—
So that I, a woman,
Can hear and obey
His loving command
To shine.

FEAR AND LOVE

Into the wilderness I
Must go.
Stripped bare…
My heart laid open
To declare myself
Broken.

Walls as thick as concrete
Keep me hidden
Impenetrable to criticisms,
Questions, and judgments.
Impenetrable too to love.

My hard outer shell is
By-product of the fear that
If I bare my soul
You'll see the unhealed emotional hole
Know that I'm just playing a role
And use that against me.

My too gruff demeanor
Cloaks the fear that
You'll pierce through my broken armor
And stab my heart till it bleeds
Leaving me to die alone
Unmourned by anyone.

I am quick to confront…
Always on the hunt
With knife blades in my voice,
Fearing you'll think me

Not worthy of your words of comfort
Should I fall.

My life is cloaked in fear
Of falling
Of failing
Of not being interesting enough
Of not being cool enough
Of not being good enough
For your time,
Your kiss, your tender thoughts.

Fear that you'll leave
That you'll not believe in me
Fear that you'll say you love me
And lie.
Fear that the distance between us
Is too vast and you will not be strong enough
To reach across
Or interested enough to try.

Fear that you won't see me
Though I raise my feathers and strut
My stuff in your presence.
Fear that you will look away
At the very moment that I smile.

Fear sprouts from
The empty places of my past:
From the men who have come only to play
The women who have rolled their eyes,
Looked me up and down,
Turned and walked away.
Friends who smiled politely

Then bared their fangs in
The market place.

Fear births
Anger
Hostility
Self-hatred.
The belief that I am not good enough
Even for God to love.

But I am.

John 4:8 says, *There is no fear in love.*
So, in the wilderness I stand
Wounds open, hurts laid bare,
Fears revealed
Waiting to feel God's hand
On my heart.
Needing so desperately to start
To live
Unmindful of what man might
Do about
Say about
Think about
Me.

Laying open my wounded soul
Begins the process to becoming whole
But not until my paralyzing fear is replaced by
The deep, abiding, solidly stable love
Of God.
It is through Him that love is made complete
And through surrender that I can

Meet Him—
Empty

Ready for His heart to beat
Inside me.

In the wilderness I stand
Ready to grasp the loving hand
Of God.

BUTTERFLY MUSINGS

Damned butterfly!
Rich yellow
Inviting me to
Watch it play.
Wings flutter
From flower to
Flower.
No time to sit
And ponder.
But I do.
I wonder where he'll
Light
Once I frighten him
Away
And why he chose this bud
On which to stop
And play.
His constant flitting
Reminds me not
To stay too long
Or get attached
For more is required
Than what one bud
Can store
And more service is
Demanded in payment
For my wings.
Damned, beautiful
Butterfly
Proving yet again
That even beauty comes
With a cost.

CATERPILLAR TO BUTTERFLY

I have been a caterpillar—
How about you?
Have you been a caterpillar too?
I mean,
I lived a caterpillar life
One fraught with
All the strife
That comes with an unreflective life.

The damage I did
In my caterpillar time
Might have been thought unforgivable
Had I not transformed from
Lowly caterpillar worm
To Holy butterfly-woman.

Locked inside
My self-imposed cocoon
Away from the complications
And busy-ness of day to day
I knelt to pray
To meditate and, at last,
slay the demons
From my caterpillar past.

In chrysalis I stayed
Contemplating in silence
Things I'd done wrong
That kept me from being strong
In my beliefs…
That kept me caterpillar wrong.
People-pleaser, that was me

Never knowing who to be
Holding on to men
Who didn't deserve me
Who never loved
Nor tried to see me.
Letting friends take advantage
Maintaining a loving image
While inside I hid
A silent caterpillar rage.

And then it happened:
I forgave.

And from the dark of my cocoon
I began the breakthrough
From which I soon
Would emerge, robust
Ready to say in God I trust.
Ready to proclaim myself
A Butter fly miracle
Ready to see myself as
Butterfly-beautiful.

I am now a butterfly—
How about you?
Aren't you a butterfly too?
We both had the courage to
Be transformed
No longer content to
Live as a lowly worm.

What people thought or said
While we were caterpillar dead
Was probably true

But we are shining examples
Of what the light of God can do.
For having experienced the darkness
Of cocoon, we have embraced
The change and light, that soon
Will prepare our wings for flight.

We've learned that *In God*
There's no darkness… only light.
So we can embrace *His Good work begun*
Knowing that He will not leave us
Until He's done.
And though our transformation is not through
Our wings have traces of freedom's hues
And now we stand ready to begin anew.

For we have combined the strength
And hope and magic of the butterfly's
Re-creation…
To fuel our needed transformation.
Now, we wait in knowing.

I believe in butterflies
Their instincts tell them
To come forth into light…
Even though that metamorphosis
Will surely cause fright.
It is in the light where their colors glow
It is in God's light where we can grow.

I believe in butterflies.
I believe in me
And you.

I'M EATING MY WAY...

I'm eating myself to distraction
It seems eating is my reaction
To all things negative in my life.
I eat out of frustration
Eat out of pain
Eat out of boredom
Or to fill my empty tank.

I'm eating because my friends moved,
Pulled away, or died.
Their absence makes me feel cast off—
Suddenly pushed aside.

I'm feeding the need for intimacy
Faking the feeling of love
Searching for my life's purpose
Eating to feel enough of.

I'm simulating passion
Filling up the emptiness:
The empty arms
The empty bed
The empty heart unfed.

I'm eating because I can't let go
The baggage of my past:
I can't forgive
Can't un-live
Those days I felt outcast.
Back then, instead of eating
I gave myself to men.

Same difference.

But, food doesn't soothe my hurt feelings
Just keeps me from seeking healing.
Numbs my feelings and keeps me dealing
Though sometimes I want to quit.

I'm eating out of guilt
I'm eating out of fear
I'm eating to keep my tears in check
I'm eating to disappear.

Or, so the experts say
But I've begun look at myself
And to think a different way:

I eat while cowering in the corner
Full of self-ridicule
Because I was given dominion over
All the earth
And have forgotten
How to rule.

A WOMAN WHO CAN

I am a woman who can.
One who can see the positive
And recognize that
Though weeping may endure for a night…
The morning can be filled with delight.
And though I am a woman who stumbles,
I can stop my fall
By taking one small forward step
Knowing that each tread takes me closer
To my sunrise
And the surprise of a new day.

I am a woman who can
Understand that some doors must close
And block my way
In order to still my ego,
Teaching me to *Let go, and let God*
Do His work in me
And making me grateful that
Things do work together for good
So, that every valley and every hill
I can count as God's will
To get me closer to spirit, and in that place,
Feel Him freeing me to be the woman
He wants me to be.

I am a woman who can love herself, flaws and all.
Recognizing that perfection belongs only to God
And, in humility, am at peace with me as His creation.
Thus, I am a woman who has
Released the past and moved forward,
Forgiving my shortcomings and my excesses,

My bad decisions and wrong turns
And have created a positive vision for my life.
I have said aloud: *I am more than a conqueror,*
And have spoken that into existence
So that my secret self has been revealed
And the dreams I dreamed
And the gifts I claimed were set free.

I decided to write my vision,
To set my plan
To encourage others
To say, Yes, I can!

Yes, I Can—
Walk a new way
Take a new path
Forget my past
And be free to unmask
The creative talents
Inside me.
Yes, I can
Rely on God's plan
For my prosperity and peace
And have hope that my service
Will help others release
The demons that have dimmed
their dreams.
For this positive Life-view
I pray: Dear Lord,
Thank you
For each new beginning
And daily chance to take my stand
And encourage others to say Yes, I can.

SOME THINGS I JUST KNOW

All it should take is birth
For a woman
To see her worth.
But, no, she has to go through
A lot of shit first.
And even then
She seems to wallow
In her shit so long
The odor fills her lungs
And she breathes the stench of —
And eventually becomes the by-product of
Her own rankness.

I mean— women can hear God calling
Offering healing
And peace
Yet we find it hard
To cease playing
That same old record
Whose scratches
Distort the sound
But, because the words are known
So well,
We don't even notice.
We just sing over
The irritating noise
And automatically poise ourselves
For the storm.

Women stay in the storm
So long

We think that's
Where we're supposed to be.
It takes a while for us to see
Our lives any other way.

If our man hits us, we think we
Deserve it
We don't muster up the nerve
To leave
Until he almost beats
Us down
Pounding us emotionally
To the ground—
Then, some of us
Go back.

If our friends betray us,
We might ask ourselves why
And we may cry
For a minute
But then we put ourselves right
Back in the drama
Where friend and enemy look
The same
And we play the game of
Who got who last, asking,
What can I do
To get that bitch back?
We tell ourselves lies about
Our looks and our smarts,
Listening too long to voices
That start when we're young.
Saying we can't do
Or be

What our hearts said back then—
Before incest and rape
Made shit of our dreams.
The voices sing their nay saying
Again and again
Until we pick up the tune
And sing on our own
That we know nothing
Have nothing
Are nothing of worth
Then we're doomed to believe
That life should hurt
Because it does.

Women dress up
And play at mother, at boss, at friend.
All the while trudging
Through the stale shit
Our lives have become
Unsure of when fear moved in,
Taking residence in our psyches
Where dreams should have been.

It seems some deep, dark awful shit
Has to hit before we admit
Our lives ought to be better than this.

ABOUT THE AUTHOR

Jackie Dove-Miller is a graduate of St. Andrews Presbyterian College (BA) and NC State University (MA). She is a retired English teacher, a poet and the founder of Spirit Of Peace, which markets inspirational novelties that feature her original prayers, poems and photos. She writes, performs and has produced a sample CD of inspirational spoken-word poetry (*A Spoken-Word For a Woman Who Can*) that focuses on women's issues that are dear to her heart. She sees her poetry as a ministry meant to help women see themselves capable of overcoming life's obstacle. She has been published in *Carolina Country, Gravity Hill Literary Magazine*, and local newspapers and arts magazines. She has recently begun facilitating workshops and seminars related to empowering women. Living in the Raleigh area with her husband, Allen Miller, Jackie loves spending time reading, writing, photography and volunteering. *Some Things I Just Know* is her first full volume of published poetry.